Smooth Transitions

Ensuring continuity from the Foundation Stage

by Ros Bayley and Sally Featherstone
Illustrated by Martha Hardy

Featherstone Education
An imprint of Bloomsbury Publishing Plc

50 Bedford Square   1385 Broadway
London   New York
WC1B 3DP   NY 10018
UK   USA

www.bloomsbury.com

Bloomsbury is a registered trade mark of Bloomsbury Publishing Plc

This edition published 2014

First published 2003

Text © Ros Bayley & Sally Featherstone, 2003
Illustrations © Martha Hardy, 2003
Cover photographs © Shutterstock

British Library Cataloguing-in-Publication Data
A catalogue record for this book is available from the British Library.

ISBN 978-1-4081-8912-2

Library of Congress Cataloging-in-Publication Data
A catalog record for this book is available from the Library of Congress.

1 3 5 7 9 10 8 6 4 2

Printed and bound in India by Replika Press Pvt. Ltd.

This book is produced using paper that is made from wood grown in managed, sustainable forests. It is natural, renewable and recyclable. The logging and manufacturing processes conform to the environmental regulations of the country of origin.

To view more of our titles please visit
www.bloomsbury.com

Smooth Transitions

Contents

Introduction

Ensuring continuity from the Foundation Stage

The Foundation Stage is a success! It is a statutory stage of education, with its own legal status and responsibilities, its own curriculum aims, structure and guidance, and its own Key Stage assessments. The Foundation Stage also has its own documentation on planning and organising an appropriate learning environment.

Most importantly, the Foundation Stage has put an emphasis on a particular learning and teaching style, based on what we know about the ways young children learn best – through:

- **active**, child-initiated learning
- planned and free access **play** activities
- an **integrated**, whole curriculum style
- **independent** and **exploratory** learning
- access to **learning outside** as well as inside
- a recognition that **boys and girls learn differently**
- **flexibility** to accommodate individual needs, events and interests
- extended periods of **time** for children to become absorbed in activities
- **a good balance** of individual, small group and large group activities
- adult intervention and assessment based on close **observation** of children's

The curriculum for all Key Stages has now been reviewed, and implementation dates are:

- for the Revised Foundation Stage Curriculum – 2012
- for the National Curriculum for Key Stages 1, 2, and 3 – 2014.

Among other things, these revisions are intended to ease transition between Key Stages and address the following tensions. Whether these aspirations will be achieved still remains to be seen:

- an active (doing) curriculum ⇆ a more passive (listening) curriculum
- an integrated curriculum ⇆ a subject based curriculum
- play based literacy/numeracy activities ⇆ literacy/numeracy 'hours'
- larger numbers of adults ⇆ smaller number of adults
- individual/small group work ⇆ large group/class activities
- child initiated activities ⇆ adult directed activities
- informal access to the outside ⇆ timetabled break/playtime
- individual child focus ⇆ whole school 'target' driven focus
- 'bottom up' influence ⇆ 'top down' influence

Everything we now know tells us that a 'bottom up' model, where the best of foundation stage practice is extended into Year 1 is more likely to be successful than over preparation of children in a 'top down' model which puts inappropriate pressure on children in Reception.

However, the responsibility for addressing these issues does not lie solely in 'changing the practice of the teachers in Key Stage 1'. It needs shared effort. Foundation Stage practitioners, parents and children themselves need to work in partnership with teachers and classroom assistants in Year 1 to ensure success in one of the most exciting and challenging changes children face.

Smooth Transitions has been written to help everyone to manage the process, while:

- preserving the best of foundation stage practice
- recognising that Key Stage 1 is different, while not making it too different too quickly
- maintaining a smooth transition where children feel secure, comfortable and successful, and change is introduced gradually
- making sure that vital information is transferred
- providing support for vulnerable children
- making sure that parents and children are involved in the process
- managing the gradual transition to more formal teaching of essential skills
- recognising the different learning styles of different children and of girls and boys
- incorporating what we now know about effective learning and teaching of 5 to 7 year olds.

The suggestions in this book offer you a menu to choose from. Some of the activities and ideas will already be familiar to you, some will be new. They have all been tried in situations where successful transition is established. We hope you will find them helpful in extending what you already do.

And finally...

A Year 1 boy at Mount Pleasant School in Dudley (where transition from the Foundation Stage to KS1 is a development priority), when asked why he didn't like being in Year 1, said after a brief pause:

"There ent no sand and the work's too 'ard."

This book is dedicated to him!

How children learn

Most of what we know about the brain and about how children learn has been discovered in the past 15 years. Scientists are now able to examine the human brain while we are alive, and the working of even very small babies' brains can be monitored without the babies being aware of what is going on. This research has led to the discovery that from birth, and even before, babies and children already know and understand far more than we once thought they did. They are not 'blank slates' for us to write on.

"Even before birth, each child has the greatest mind that has ever existed, each child is the most powerful learning machine in the universe. Every young child has the potential, the instinct and the ability to learn."

How Babies Think, Gopnik et al.

We now know that the human baby is born with more than 100 billion brain cells, each capable of making 20,000 connections with other cells. And we know that babies and young children make learning connections in their brains faster and better in an enriched environment. This does not mean we should play them Mozart, use flash cards or buy special programmes for learning. It means that children flourish best in an environment which is exciting, engaging, and full of adults who are interested in them – an environment where every sense is stimulated.

"The richer the sensory environment and the greater our freedom to explore it, the more intricate will be the patterns for learning, thought and creativity."

Smart Moves, Carla Hannaford

We also know (from brain scans of living children) that a three year old's brain is twice as active as an adult brain, and this level of activity continues until the age of nine or ten. Young children's brains are more active, more connected, and much more flexible than ours.

We know that children develop 50% of their eventual ability to learn (sometimes described as their intelligence) before the age of four, and another 30% before they are eight.

We also know that adult interaction and physical activity continue to make a massive difference to learning during childhood.

"To learn anything effectively you have to see it, hear it and feel it."
Tony Stockwell in 'The Learning Revolution'

"In order for learning to take place, children's bodies must take part in physical experience.'"
'Rhythms of Learning', Brewer and Campbell

"Good outcomes for children are linked to adult-child interactions which involve 'sustained shared thinking' and open ended questioning."
EPPE Project, DfES

Boys and girls

What do we know about the differences between girls and boys?

From birth, boys and girls are different and their brains develop in different ways. When a baby is born he or she has made relatively few links between the two hemispheres, or sides of the brain. As soon as babies are born, and in response to each experience, they begin to build on these links, making more dendrites (connections) between the neurons in their brains.

Nutrition, stimulation, touch, taste, smell, hearing all contribute to the process, and the richer the environment the faster the baby will make the links. From as early as six weeks, boys will tend to concentrate on developing the right half of their brain (the half that deals with objects), while girls tend to concentrate on the left half (the half that deals with faces and sounds). Experienced practitioners will know that when children enter their setting, girls are still generally more interested in people and how they work, boys are still more interested in things and how they work.

We now have evidence that girls will usually choose activities that involve (or are near) an adult. Girls watch adults closely and model their behaviour. In role play, girls are likely to imitate adults (their mothers, older siblings, and the practitioners in the setting). It is girls who invent games about doing the register, organising snack and mealtimes, going shopping, cleaning up. Their play is often uncannily accurate, and we sometimes see and hear ourselves repeated with embarrassing accuracy by the girls we work with! Most girls have made sufficient links in their brains to begin the complex skills of reading and writing by the time they are four and a half, while in most boys it is nearer six. As Early Years practitioners we need to use this knowledge as we work.

Before a child can learn the complex skills of reading and writing, they need to make hundreds of thousands of links between their left brain and right brain, through the 'super highway' of the brain called the corpus callosum.

In order to develop these essential links between left and right brain hemispheres, children need to be involved in activities using both sides of their bodies – both hands, both feet, both eyes, both ears. Rhythmic stamping, clapping, hopping and skipping, climbing ladders and swinging on ropes, riding bikes and scooting scooters all help this development. Throwing and catching, hitting and bouncing balls also help; so does work in construction, dough, cutting and model-making. Many practitioners are adding brain gym, movement rhymes, and drinking water to their sessions, knowing that these stimulate the brain, too.

Researchers have found that, from their first days in school, most boys will choose activities that do not involve an adult.

They will also choose to be outside for a large portion of the day, involved in action-packed, practical tasks with frequent changes of activity. Girls stay nearer to adults, watching what they are doing. They will more often choose books, drawing or painting, and from as young as four, girls spend twice as long on an activity as boys. Four year old boys change their activities five times as often as girls, and by this age, most are able to concentrate for less than five minutes on an activity.

We now have support from research all over the world, which tells us that young children learn best from doing, and boys are the supreme 'doers'. If we want to help boys to succeed in our Foundation Stage settings and in Key Stage 1, we must defend their rights to develop through an active curriculum, where mark-making, drawing and writing can emerge naturally in their favourite habitat: the stimulating and action packed environment, indoors and out, where practitioners have planned a curriculum which takes the inside out, presenting all activities in a first-hand environment.

■ Four key apects

Everything we now know about the development of the brain is consistent with the guidance for the Foundation Stage. What we must now do is continue that knowledge into Key Stage 1 and use it to shape how we teach, rather that what we teach, so we ensure children learn what they need and learn how to learn.

"What we need is the inventive intelligence and the will to make sure that babies and young children can exercise their innate ability to learn and that adults, not just mothers but all of us, can exercise our equally innate ability to teach them."
Gopnik et al.

Four key aspects in putting the research into practice for successful transition are:

■ **Space**
■ **Time**
■ **People**
■ **Information**

The four aspects, activities that are linked to them and issues that might arise are considered in detail on the following pages.

■ **Space**

Children of five and six years old need space that meets their learning needs. When children move from Foundation Stage to Key Stage 1, careful consideration will need to be given to the arrangement of the physical space to ensure that there is continuity of experience between the two phases. Key Stage 1 staff will need to spend time looking at the key features of the learning environment in the reception class, and observe the way in which it is being used by the children. Once this has happened, they will be able to decide how to make developmentally appropriate provision for the autumn term; provision that supports a smooth join between the two experiences.

This process is absolutely crucial, and unless it takes place, it is highly likely that when children enter Key Stage 1 they will enter an environment that has a negative effect on both their well-being and their learning.

Before transfer, try some of these:

■ Build the environment in time for Key Stage 1 staff to observe the children as they move about and use the learning space in their Reception class.

■ Create time for the staff in Reception and Key Stage 1 to discuss the learning needs of the children together.

■ Talk with the children about their expectations of their new learning environment.

■ Consider how each aspect of this learning environment can be continued in Key Stage 1 – sand, water, construction, role play, etc.

■ Think about how you can build progression into each aspect, i.e. putting the same basic provision in place, while at the same time ensuring that you have added enough new materials to allow the children to work at an increased level of complexity.

■ Think back to the things you enjoyed doing when you were five or six. The things that young children enjoy and learn from today are not so very different, and if you do spend time on this simple exercise you will be amazed to see how many of those memorable activities involved the use of large spaces and active movement, and how many of them happened outside!

Before and during transfer we need to spend time considering ways in which we give children access to large spaces and outdoor experiences.

Some of the questions we need to ask ourselves include the following. Do we:

- Make a conscious effort to build such experiences into the weekly and daily plans?
- Think about how we can make the best possible use of the school grounds?
- Have a range of prop boxes, bags and other resources that can be taken outside with the minimum amount of fuss?
- Look at the ways in which we might use the hall when it is not being used by the rest of the school?
- Identify those children who need high levels of physical activity (usually boys) and make special provision for them?

As part of designing an appropriate learning environment, have we thought about how the children will use the space?

Some of the issues that may arise are:

- Building in time to introduce children to their new environment, showing them how to use it and sharing our expectations with them.
- Ensuring that children can take care of their own needs by accessing resources and materials and putting them away again.
- Giving children responsibility for caring for their new environment.
- Structuring the timetable in such a way that children have continued and frequent opportunities for child-initiated learning, and plenty of time to extend their activities.

Once we have made decisions about what will be the most appropriate learning environment for Key Stage 1 children, consider:

- Have we communicated with the rest of the staff about why we have made the decisions we have made?
- Have we checked out the expectations of the parents? There might be an expectation that Year 1 is not the sort of place where you would find sand, water or role-play activities!
- Have we set up a meeting with parents where we can explain the importance of an active learning environment?

■ Time

Children and adults need time for the transfer process to be successful:

"Children develop and learn in different ways and at different rates."
Revised Framework for the EYFS

For any new experience to be turned into learning, children need time to become familiar with the new situation, getting used to what will be different and what will be the same. If we leave this adjusting till the autumn, we leave the children all summer to think, worry and imagine what it will be like. Worry results in stress, and stress inhibits learning. Stressed children are also more likely to be tired, aggressive and impulsive. Some will become withdrawn and distracted.

Before and during transfer, do we give children the following opportunities?

- ■ Time in their new classroom or school before the summer holiday.

- ■ Time to talk about the new place, the new people and the new programme.

- ■ Time to think about what they have learned in Reception or Nursery, what they know and can do, and the things they are good at.

- ■ Time to find out about what will be the same – friends, family, activities – as well as what will be different.

- ■ Time to absorb the information, check the details, and go back for another look (through photos or further visits).

- ■ Time to share experiences with the present Key Stage 1 children – outings, visits in both directions, letters and messages, photos.

In Key Stage 1, before we make judgements about what children know and can do, do we give them these opportunities?

- ■ Time to learn the new routines and procedures.

- ■ Time to adjust to new activities.

- ■ Time to make new friends.

- ■ Time to get to know new adults.

- ■ Time with activities that are familiar, to remember and revisit what they know and can do.

- ■ Sustained lengths of time to play, to select their own activities, to make friends, to be out side, to talk, to be active.

And what do the adults involved in transfer need time for?

During the summer term, some of these ideas might help:

- Take time to enjoy the last term with the children and celebrate what they have learned with you.
- Take time to watch the children, identifying those who might need some additional support at transfer.
- Take time to talk to and about each child as an individual.
- Take time to think about the information you are sending.
- Take time to help the children and their parents manage a significant change.

During the first weeks of the autumn term, do we give ourselves and other adults the following opportunities?

- Time to get to know the children and their families.
- Time to read the information that has been offered by colleagues and parents.
- Time to find out what children already know.
- Time to watch children in play activities chosen by themselves.
- Time to think about how to manage the transition in planning and organising the curriculum from Reception to Key Stage 1.
- Time to notice and support those children who may find the transition to a more formal curriculum difficult (particularly summer born children, those with EAL or SEN, children who have disturbing or disturbed behaviour, and many of the boys).
- Time to read what the curriculum guidance says about the move between the Reception and Year 1 programmes.

The revised curriculum promotes:

"Pupils entering Year 1 who have not yet met the early learning goals for literacy should continue to follow the curriculum for the Early Years Foundation Stage to develop their word reading, spelling and language skills. However, these pupils should follow the Year 1 programme of study in terms of the books they listen to and discuss, so that they develop their vocabulary and understanding of grammar, as well as their knowledge more generally across the curriculum."

Programme of Study for Year 1;
Revised National Curriculum 2014

■ Key aspect 3

■ **People**

Children need people who have a clear understanding of why the transfer process needs to be handled sensitively and thoughtfully. No matter how good your transition policy, it's people who have to make it work, and by paying attention to a few simple principles, difficulties can be minimised and misunderstandings avoided. When people fully understand why decisions have been taken, and feel that they have been consulted about and involved in the decision-making process, outcomes are much more likely to be successful.

Before the transfer process takes place, take time to set up a meeting between senior management, Reception and Key Stage 1 practitioners where you can all engage in a dialogue about how you will handle this important transition. Make sure there is plenty of time for discussion and you can really do justice to this important debate.

If you are the person responsible for managing the transfer, before the meeting make some notes of the issues which need to be discussed. Acknowledge to all concerned that this is **not** an easy process but that by making your decisions on the basis of evidence about how young children learn, you will be doing your best for everyone concerned. Make sure that everyone taking part in the debate is fully briefed about the most recent research into brain development.

Before the transfer, plan some time to:

- ■ Talk with the children about their move to Key Stage 1. Encourage them to share their thoughts and feelings about the move.

- ■ Reassure them if they express concerns. Acknowledge their feelings and help them to understand that new situations can sometimes be a little scary!

- ■ Ask them about how they would like the move to happen. (You'll be amazed at what they'll come up with!)

- ■ Involve children in making preparations for the move; e.g. collecting together and packing up anything that is going to be taken with them.

- ■ Involve children in making labels and captions for displays in their new classroom.

- Involve children in making a display of photographs with information about themselves that can be put up in the new classroom for the Key Stage 1 staff.
- Show children where they will put their personal things in their new classroom. Let them make their own new labels.
- Brief them about the daily routine, especially where it differs from their present one.

Throughout the summer term, communicate with the parents about how transition is being handled. Consider whether it might be helpful to:

- Hold a meeting where you share your thinking.
- Consult with them about their aspirations, expectations and concerns.
- Give a presentation about the most recent research into brain development and how young children learn most effectively.
- Talk with them about the negative consequences of putting children under pressure to work too formally too soon.
- Encourage them to think about the sorts of things they were doing when they were the same age as their children are now!

Before the transfer, take time to consider whether it would be possible to have some mobility of staffing between Reception and Key Stage 1. This would enable the Key Stage 1 staff to get to know the children **before** the transfer.

Alternatively, during the first weeks of the autumn term, would it be possible for a classroom assistant or nursery nurse to move **with** the children to support them through the move?

Information on brain development can be found in:

The Thinking Child; Nicola Call with Sally Featherstone, 2011

and

Learning to Learn from Birth to Five; Sally Featherstone, 2014.

Both titles from Bloomsbury.

■ Information

Adults, children and their families need helpful information before, during and after transition. Each group needs a different sort of information, and at different times.

In the previous sections we have covered many of the purposes and audiences for transfer information, suggesting ways in which you can collect and offer this vital information at the right time, to the right people.

Whenever and however this information is needed, it must give everyone CONFIDENCE in the success of the process. Information must be:

Concise – manageable amounts in a manageable form

Organised – so that the receiving teacher can make sense of it

Non judgemental – giving unbiased, objective information

Family friendly – honest, open and jargon-free

Individual – celebrating each individual child

Digestible – given in manageable, timely installments

Evidence based – judgements resulting from observation

Nationally moderated – incorporating the Foundation Profile

Convertible – easily translated into National Curriculum terms

Encompassing – recognising and celebrating the whole child and the whole curriculum.

Look at what you collect and what you give to others.
Does your information pass the CONFIDENCE test?

Finally in this section, we offer some thoughts on the sorts of statistical and more formal information which might usefully be communicated between the Foundation Stage and Year 1.

Following consultation and the review of the Foundation Stage curriculum, the Foundation Stage Profile was reviewed and updated in 2013. The revised Profile:

- Covers progress in the Reception Year.

- Has 17 statements relating to the seven areas of learning and development.

- Is completed after observation of learning.

- Can be used as the Annual Report to Parents.

- Contains information which can easily be displayed in a simple spreadsheet (as long as you understand what the numbers refer to!).

Foundation Stage practitioners must make sure that their Key Stage 1 colleagues know what the Profile contains, and understand the other information which has been added to the statutory scale points.

Ideally, adults should spend time together discussing each child's profile before they move into Key Stage 1, so the new teacher can use the information to:

- Establish **starting points** for each child.

- Identify children who may have **additional learning needs** (including SEN and EAL).

- Identify children who may be **gifted or talented** in one or more areas of the curriculum.

- Identify children who need a **modified curriculum** – more 'Foundation-like' and active – these may include summer born children and boys.

- Identify children who have had a **disrupted, disadvantaged or 'turbulent'** time in the Foundation Stage.

- Get a 'feel' of the unique **nature of the cohort** and how this cohort might differ from other years.

The Foundation Profile passes the CONFIDENCE test if everyone understands it, knows how to interpret what it says, and is involved in making it work. The Profile is only worth doing if it helps children, their teachers and their parents. We owe it to the children to make it work for them!

Teaching CLEVER

CLEVER teaching is about using everything we already know and everything we are finding out about how children learn to help in our work.

CLEVER people doing a difficult job deserve all the help they can get!

■ CLEVER teaching is:

Child-centred

A curriculum which is child-centred and takes into account all we know about the ways children develop will help CLEVER teaching. We must continue to develop our own professional knowledge to ensure this.

Learning (not teaching) focused

A focus on learning, rather than teaching, will enable us to to concentrate on the activities and methods which meet children's needs. We will not waste time on methods or activities which are 'empty' of learning.

Engaging

People, places, objects and activities that engage children's interests, enthusiasms and enjoyment will ensure CLEVER teaching. We now have much more information about what engages children, and what doesn't!

Value-based

CLEVER teaching values children, their unique qualities and contributions. Children who value themselves and know they are valued will be more motivated and will learn more.

Efficient and effective

A clear focus on children's learning, and teaching methods which support learning, will ensure efficient use of time, space, resources and people. CLEVER teaching ensures effectiveness, not just efficiency.

Realistic

CLEVER teaching will focus on what children can and should be doing, rather than the things they can't. It ensures a focus on 'sustained shared thinking' in the real world – a realistic approach to teaching and learning.

Child-centred learning

Teachers of young children have always been able to see the relevance of a child-centred curriculum, which has real meaning and significance to the young learner. They have always understood intuitively that such a curriculum is one through which young children can learn with engagement, excitement and success. Starting with the child has always made sense, but over the last decade we have learned so much from research into brain development that we now have evidence to support what we have always intuitively known! The Revised Statutory Framework for the EYFS states that:

*"Children learn and develop well in **enabling environments**, in which their experiences respond to their individual needs and there is a strong partnership between practitioners and parents and/or carers."*

In planning a developmentally appropriate curriculum for children entering Key Stage 1, this research is not only vitally important in our teaching, it also gives us the ammunition we need to counter arguments for a more formal and less appropriate provision.

We now know that:

- It is not so much a matter of how many brain cells we are genetically endowed with, as the degree to which those brain cells are stimulated by early experiences.

- Brain cells can only become usable intelligence when they are connected to each other. How effectively these neural connections are made is hugely dependent on the learning environment in which we grow.

- During the first five to six years of life, some 50 per cent of the brain's nerve cells are connected, forming the basis for future learning.

Resource note:

Documents available from **www.education.gov.uk** or **www.foundationyears.org.uk/early-years-foundation-stage-2012**

We also know that:

- **Connections** between the brain cells are not always 'positive'. A child pressured into too much formality too soon can form 'negative' connections, resulting in negative attitudes and dispositions towards learning. Negative attitudes formed at this stage in someone's life can become virtually indelible!

- Some children will not have developed the **optimal binocular vision** essential for reading until the age of seven or eight. The same can be true for the motor skill coordination necessary for writing.

- Involving the **emotional brain** in the learning process is essential if learning is to be memorable.

- Young children **learn best** through active, multi-sensory experiences.

- Children need **periods of relaxation** in which to consolidate and practise what they have learned.

- **Movement** is essential to learning.

As Carla Hannaford says in her book 'Smart Moves':

"The more closely we consider the elaborate interplay of brain and body, the more one compelling theme emerges: movement is essential to learning. Movement awakens and activates our mental capacities. Movement integrates and anchors new information and experience into our neural networks. And movement is vital to all the actions by which we embody and express our learning, our understanding of ourselves."

Resource note:

Smart Moves; Great Ocean Publishers, 2005

As CLEVER practitioners, we need to have confidence that, in planning active learning experiences for children in Key Stage 1, we are giving them exactly what they need to be motivated, enthusiastic and successful learners. Failure to do this can only result in children becoming demotivated, disenchanted and 'switched off' – maybe for ever!

When planning learning experiences for young children, we need to build in opportunities for as much movement as possible. On an adult-initiated activity, the average five-year old can concentrate for a period of time roughly equal to double their age, so remember that three short sessions will be more productive than one long one. In addition:

- Plan for brain breaks that give children the opportunity to move as soon as they begin to get restless. This may involve the use of some 'Brain Gym' exercises, or simply playing a game of 'Simon Says' or 'Heads, Shoulders, Knees and Toes.'
- Use kinesthetic teaching programmes like 'Write Dance'. This excellent handwriting programme teaches all the basic movements for handwriting through gross motor movement, and is stimulating, exciting and fun to implement.
- Make every possible use of the outside area and the hall. Where this is not possible, consciously think about how you can maximise the amount of movement in every session.

(See page 43 for practical ideas on how to do this.)

Resource note:

Write Dance; **www.sagepub.com/education**

Implications for learning and teaching

So where does all of this leave us in terms of what we actually do with the children, and in this current 'climate of push,' is it possible to plan an active, developmentally-appropriate curriculum that matches the learning needs of children transferring to Key Stage 1? We think it is, and that if we teach CLEVER, we can achieve as much – and more – than if we allow ourselves to be railroaded into too much formality too soon! As practitioners we need to fully understand what is meant by the term 'active learning', and ensure that we plan experiences for children that are grounded in an understanding of its influence.

Active learning:

- ■ Requires that children have direct and immediate experience of objects, people, ideas and events, and the opportunity and support to derive meaning from these experiences through reflection.

- ■ Has its foundations in 'doing.' It involves handling, changing things, moving, making things – not just looking. Action is climbing, pretending, modelling, discovering and comparing. It is touching, tasting, feeling and exploring.

- ■ Has four critical elements:

    - ■ direct action on objects;
    - ■ reflection on actions;
    - ■ invention; and
    - ■ problem solving.

An active learning environment should provide daily opportunities for children to engage in all these processes.

CLEVER teachers need to check that planning enables children to:

1. Interact with materials (these should be sufficient for each child engaged in the activity).

2. Use, manipulate and explore the materials.

3. Make choices about how they work with the materials.

4. Use language while they are working with the materials.

5. Have the support of an interested adult to encourage 'sustained shared thinking'.

Learning (not teaching) focused

By putting the emphasis on learning rather than teaching, we ensure that children really are getting what they need to learn effectively. This makes demands on everyone who comes into contact with the child. As adults we should:

■ Set aside time to observe children, so that we can answer the all-important question: *Where are these children on the continuum of development and what do they need from us, right now, in order to move on in their learning?*

■ Look to see **how** children are learning: *What are their dominant learning styles and how can we ensure that we are developing all their senses through a multi-sensory approach to learning? Do the activities we plan for the children support visual, auditory and kinesthetic learning styles?*

The neocortex (the part of the brain responsible for thinking) is divided into lobes, or parts, and each one has a different function (for example, vision, hearing, touch and speech), which means that we receive sensory information and store sensory memories in different places in our brains.

Therefore, if we want to remember something easily and vividly, it makes sense to input the information in more than one lobe. In other words, CLEVER teachers should plan experiences that allow children to:

SEE IT
HEAR IT
DO IT
SAY IT

... it is then much more likely that they will have **GOT IT!**

Getting the beat

When planning for children's learning, we should also take account of the most recent research into beat competency.

It is interesting to note that the ability to maintain a steady beat appears to be necessary to successfully perform any task that involves sophisticated movement. We need this sense of timing when walking, dancing, writing, cutting with scissors, hammering in a nail or drawing. In fact, it is so essential that if someone lacks beat awareness, he or she usually has difficulties with both gross and fine motor skills.

Recent studies have also shown a correlation between beat competency and school achievement that exceeds either social class or the mother's education (the usual predictors of school success), and it is an area we can influence. By helping children to develop beat competency we can improve their chances of success!

In the light of this research, which will come as no surprise to most Early Years teachers, practitioners need to:

- Plan frequent opportunities for singing, dancing, rapping and playing musical instruments.

- Use jingles and rhymes throughout the daily routine.

For example, at the beginning of sessions you might use a rhyme like this:

Put one hand on your head and one on your nose
Now touch your head and touch your toes
Wiggle your fingers and tap your knees
Now you are ready and looking at me!

At transition times you may like to try the following:

Now its time to learn some more
So have a quick wriggle (allow time)
And thump the floor (4 times)
Then fold your arms and look this way
To show you are ready to hear what I say.

You will find that once you have used these rhymes a few times the children will soon be joining in, and it will have the joint benefits of focusing their attention and improving their sense of steady beat. You will also find that they will begin to make up their own rhymes.

Other activities that are useful for developing beat competency are:

■ Beating out a steady beat with two sticks (chopsticks are useful for this purpose).

■ Using the chopsticks to beat out a steady beat on paper plates.

■ Drumming with the hands on upturned plastic waste paper baskets (cheaper and much less noisy than conventional drums!).

■ Manipulating a bean bag to a steady beat. For example, "Put the beanbag on your head and on your nose and on your foot and on your toes"; "Put the beanbag on your elbow and your shoulder and your ankle and your heel", etc. (The adult gives these instructions to a steady beat.)

No-one is yet entirely sure why these types of steady beat activities can have such a profoundly positive effect on children's learning, although it is believed by some researchers that such activities help to integrate the left and right hemispheres of the brain, leading to more effective 'whole brain' learning.

When thinking about how children in Year 1 learn most effectively, it also becomes necessary to look at the child's need to repeat and practise activities in order to consolidate what they have learned.

CLEVER teachers need to ask themselves:

■ Once we have introduced children to an experience, have we built in opportunities for them to return to that experience?

■ Will those same materials and resources be available for further exploration and have we allocated time for such repetition to take place?

■ Have we allowed for the fact that some children will need to do this more than others? (For example, kinesthetic learners take longer to process information than auditory or visual learners.)

- To what extent are we supporting children as they reflect on what they have learned and how they have learned it? By helping children to ask themselves how a given task is going, how they could have done it better and what they might learn from the experience, we will really be helping them to become more effective learners.

- Do we talk with the children about the things they like to do best and the things they think they are best at?

- Do we, as adults, reflect sufficiently on how we have presented material to the children, and ask ourselves whether we allowed enough time for exploration, understanding and memorisation?

- Do we explore ways in which we could have done things more effectively?

- Do we build in enough periods of relaxation? (The brain does not function well when it is stressed or overworked!)

- Have we thought about carrying out some relaxation or visualisation exercises with the children to help them to get the brain into the right 'state' for learning?

And, as part of our focus on learning, we need to ask ourselves:

- Have the children got the key skills necessary for effective learning?

- How good are their expressive language skills? (We all know that effective speakers make effective readers and writers!)

- Have the children got the listening skills for effective learning?

- How good are their memory skills?

- How well are they able to concentrate on a given task, and for what period of time?

- How good is their basic concept development?

- How developed is their phonological awareness?

If, having posed these questions, we have concerns in any of these areas – and it will be most likely that we will – we will then need devise programmes which address these issues in engaging, multisensory, active and fun ways. You may find the following books helpful:

Child Initiated Learning; Ros Bayley and Sally Featherstone

Foundations for Independence; Ros Bayley and Sally Featherstone

Thinking Child; Nicola Call and Sally Featherstone

Supporting Child Initiated Learning; ed. Sally Featherstone

All available from Bloomsbury.

Engaging the learner

Engaging learners is the central purpose of our teaching. To engage every child we need to engage all sorts of learners, all sorts of interests and counter all sorts of distractions and pressures. There are three major ways in which we learn:

- Some of us learn mostly by using our eyes **(visual learners)**.
- Some of us learn mostly by using our hearing **(auditory learners)**.
- Some of us learn mostly by using the sense of touch and experiencing movement **(kinaesthetic learners)**.

Some children learn almost exclusively in one of these three ways.

The visual learner: We have all met children who need to be engaged by the picture in a story – who need to see the story happening. They need help to visualise what we are saying. These children benefit from the use of puppets, pictures and objects. They will recall learning by 'seeing it again' and remembering what things look like.

The auditory learner: We have also all met children who look away when we tell the same story, apparently not listening, but able to retell the story in elaborate detail when asked! These are auditory learners and they sometimes need to look away so they can hear more clearly without distracting pictures or movement. Auditory learners benefit from sounds or music to accompany their learning. They often listen or think with their eyes closed.

The kinaesthetic learner: The third sort of familiar child is the one who must touch to learn. Their hands go out to each object or piece of equipment. They need to feel their learning through their skin, and benefit from the use of tactile materials and real objects. They also learn well through movement, walking through a story or experience, and demonstrating in movement or signs.

We can all recognise the children who are predominantly one of the three sorts of learner. Other children may have a preference at a particular stage, they may move through phases of a predominant style, or they may never develop a predominant learning style, using a combination of two or all three.

The Foundation Stage provides an ideal setting for meeting the needs of different styles of learning, and practitioners can more easily respond to children's preferences. They have space, including outdoors, they have time, they often have more adults, and therefore more opportunities to work in small groups, planned to meet individual needs. There is more flexibility to respond to incidental opportunities for learning, and to give children more time to explore the environment. And, of course, everyone expects the Reception or Nursery classroom to be active, lively and full of visual stimulation!

The Year 1 teacher may have fewer of these benefits, and the expectation from their managers may be that 'things should be different in Key Stage 1'.

If Year 1 children are going to stay engaged with learning, it is vital that teachers resist the downward pressure, maintain a flexible approach to the curriculum, and become more aware of the different learners in their class. Teachers should also try to monitor their own teaching to ensure that they do not use a style which only appeals to one type of learner (a teacher will have a tendency to teach in the style they favour for learning!).

Some things that help CLEVER teachers:

- Finding out more about learning styles.

- Asking the Reception teachers how they ensure engagement of all the children – go and watch them working.

- Checking your planning and make sure you use all the different styles of teaching during the day or over a week.

- Using props, music, brain gym, movement and other ways to engage children's attention.

- Adopting a more flexible approach to learning in the Autumn term of Year 1 by using the guidance for the EYFS, particularly for those children who have not reached the Early Learning Goals.

"The impact of date of birth on cognitive test scores is well documented across many countries, with the youngest children in each academic year performing more poorly, on average, than the older members of their cohort."

When you are Born Matters; Claire Crawford et al; Institute for Fiscal Studies, 2011

It is a good idea to use a simple observation in order to find out the preferred learning styles of the children in your class. Learning styles can change over time, so it is useful to check regularly (perhaps once every year).

To identify their major learning style, you need to ask each child to recall something or somewhere they know well (e.g. their bedroom, a recent event, a place or person they know well). As the child talks and thinks, watch their eyes:

- Visual learners tend to look up as they recall and talk

- Auditory learners tend to look to the side

- Kinaesthetic learners tend to look down.

Another factor in securing engagement of learners is the environment in which they learn.

The engaging environment is:

- familiar but not boring *(giving children confidence, but with occasional surprises, clear instructions and consistent management)*.

- well organised *(with clear places for things, including places for unfinished projects, good labelling and easy access)*.

- personalised *(so children have places to keep their own things)*.

- easily tidied by children *(with child-sized cleaning tools, open shelves, clear organisation of resources)*.

- well resourced *(with plentiful supplies of equipment and ideas for their flexible use)*.

- full of interest *(with interactive displays, unusual objects and items to handle and explore)*.

- inviting *(with areas to be quiet, to be noisy, to be active, to reflect, to be with friends)*.

- flexible *(giving opportunities for children to move and re-organise furniture, equipment and resources as they work, and choices of what, where, how and who to work with)*.

Engaging teaching is the final piece in this jigsaw! How do we ensure that teaching is as engaging as it can be for every child, for as much of the time as possible?

Here is a collection of suggestions for your consideration. They are based on things that have worked for other teachers. They are equally suitable for Reception and Key Stage 1, for all CLEVER teachers.

Remember that:

- Children's concentration spans range from a minute for every year of their age (in adult-directed activities) to at least half an hour (in child-initiated activities). In small and large group times, break up the session with brain gym, movement, thinking time, prediction and other changes of focus.

- If you use music, puppets, pictures, rhymes, songs and objects, you will be capturing all three learning styles.

- If you encourage children to use all their senses, (sight, hearing, touch, taste and smell) they will remember more of what they learn.

- If you use different voices – not just in stories, but in all your teaching – you will capture and retain attention.

- Specific feedback will reward children in a way they can understand – 'Good sitting', 'Good listening', 'Careful moving', 'Good thinking', 'Good working together'. This will be much more effective than non-specific praise.

- Research identifies 'sustained shared thinking' as one of the most powerful learning tools. Discussions in small groups, and the company of interested adults will give children opportunities for this.

- Open questioning is a powerful tool for learning – 'Why do you think...?'; 'What do you think...?'; 'How does it...?'

- 'Can you think of a way to...?' – open questions cannot result in one-word answers!

- And remember that children need time to absorb, practise and revisit activities, preferably in play situations in an engaging environment.

Value-based

(Valuing children and their achievements)

 Valuing children and their achievements is absolutely fundamental to the 'teach CLEVER' approach, for the simple reason that when we feel valued, we learn more effectively! Consequently, it is in everybody's interest for us to explore the extent to which children are able to feel valued in our individual settings. Enabling children to feel valued does not happen by accident. It is complex and subtle, and whilst some adults **are** intuitively able to really value children, we can all do it much more effectively if we think consciously about what we are doing.

Before transfer, and throughout the year, we need to ensure that all adults working with the children have a common perception and a shared vision for how they will support children so that they feel valued, develop strong self-esteem and gain a positive image of themselves as learners.

Helping children to do these things is just like helping them to learn anything else, and to do it effectively we must plan for it systematically and explicitly.

Adults will need to think about the classroom ethos and consider:

- The expectations that will be placed upon children. These will vary according to children's levels of well-being. When you actively spend time doing this you will soon identify the children most in need of support in this area.

- The ways in which they listen to children, and whether some children may need more listening time than others.

- The way they operate as role models. Children learn far more from what they see us do than from the things we say. In this case, actions really do speak louder than words, so we need to demonstrate that we value ourselves!

- The extent to which children will be consulted and involved in organisational decisions about such things as classroom routines and rules. *The more the children are involved, the greater the possibilities for generating successful experiences!*

Adults should also consider:

▪ How they will create a classroom culture based on cooperation rather than competition. In a competitive culture, certain children will always feel undervalued.

▪ The ways in which children are encouraged to act independently and take responsibility. If adults hold all the power and control, children cannot begin to take responsibility for themselves. We learn to be responsible by being given responsibility.

▪ The ways in which children can be involved in caring for the environment, equipment and personal possessions.

▪ The strategies they will use to deal with any incidents of conflict or challenging behaviour. Do adults actively spend time teaching children the conflict resolution process?

▪ The extent to which risk-taking and problem-solving are encouraged. Problem-solving is a key learning skill.

▪ The methods that will be employed to support children to develop a 'can-do' attitude. *In order to do this adults will need to clarify their attitudes to 'failure.' We need to work really hard to help children to see that making mistakes and getting things wrong is a massively important part of the learning process. We need to help them to see that there is no such thing as failure... there is simply an outcome, and if we are not happy with the outcome we change what we do until we get a different result!*

To help children understand risk-taking and coping with failure, adults need to:

▪ Share their own experiences of failure with the children.

▪ Support and encourage children when things don't work out, helping them to tolerate uncertainty.

▪ Talk with the children about how important it is to be able to make mistakes and learn from them.

▪ Consciously acknowledge the efforts of children who have shown persistence in the face of outcomes they didn't want or expect.

How will we value children when planning the Key Stage 1 curriculum?

Children will benefit hugely when adults set time aside to consider:

- The way in which they give feedback to children. *Feedback should be descriptive rather than evaluative, focussing on what the child has actually achieved and involving the child in identifying growing points and next steps.*

- How children will be encouraged to set realistic, achievable goals for themselves. This is probably **the** most important part of creating an achievement culture!

- How **all** children's achievements will be celebrated. *Perhaps through a display board in the classroom, or as part of a celebration meeting, circle time or in a PSE lesson.*

- How we will support children in valuing each other and celebrating each other's achievements.

When planning the curriculum, adults need to seek out opportunities to support children in valuing themselves:

- In English, when they are discussing stories about other children.

- In D&T: designing and making products provides children with opportunities to identify different goals and means to these goals. As they make decisions on the way to achieving the goals, they are able to see themselves as powerful and capable.

- In History, as children learn about famous people, they can be encouraged to think about the skills and qualities that made these people famous. They can be encouraged to see these qualities in themselves.

- In Geography, children can be given opportunities to value themselves as they study their locality and look at the ways in which they can make a contribution to improving it.

- In music, dance, role play and drama, children can express their own feelings, and appreciate their own and others' strengths and qualities.

- In PE, children can have opportunities to participate as part of a team and begin to understand the ways in which they can make a contribution to that team.

- In Personal and Social Education children can learn about feelings and relationships and begin to see how understanding our emotions can help us to make positive choices and decisions.

When planning the broader curriculum, adults need to ensure that:

- Through circle time, children have opportunities to explore their feelings, beliefs and values and those of others, and alleviate fears about speaking in public.

- Children have opportunities to explore feelings, and further understand themselves through role-play situations.

- There are opportunities for children to gain in self-confidence by talking about the things that matter to them.

- Children have the opportunity to contribute to fund-raising activities for charity, support local community activities and groups, and develop citizenship skills.

- In particular, ensure that all staff working in the classroom have the necessary skills to support children in valuing themselves.

Resource note:

Circle Time for the Very Young; Margaret Collins
Here We go Round; Jenny Moseley
The Little Book of Circle Time; Dawn Roper
Penny Tassoni's Practical EYFS Handbook
The Reception Year in Action; Anna Ephgrave
Learning to Learn, Birth to Eight; Sally Featherstone

Efficient and effective

Efficient = doing things right
Effective = doing the right things

CLEVER teaching ensures that we are not just efficient (covering the curriculum, reaching personal and school targets, implementing national strategies, keeping children safe) but that we are also effective (doing these things in the right way, so children are learning as much as possible, using their individual skills and aptitudes, applying their learning in different situations, and learning how to learn).

It is possible to be very efficient without being effective – to do everything right, but without doing the right things. Everything we are learning about children's brains suggests these are some of 'the right things':

- Support **connection**, not disconnection

- Enable **activity**, not passivity

- Value and teach **skills** and **attributes**, not just knowledge

- Keep children **doing**, not just listening

- Establish **talking** before writing

- Encourage **thinking skills**, not just absorption

- Ensure continuing **engagement** with experiences, people, things

- Plan for **learning**, not just teaching.

CLEVER teachers make best use of all the resources, information and skills available to help them in their work. They review these regularly to ensure the most efficient and the most effective way of managing and deploying these resources.
And they are particularly vigilant when planning their work with a new group of children.

They read and use all the information provided by the previous setting, making sure they do not waste time collecting information twice.

CLEVER teachers also:

■ Spend time getting to know the new children, establishing starting points and recognising that some children may have changed during the long summer holiday – learning may have moved on since the last assessment, and some recent learning may have been lost.

■ Ensure that children have a sense of continuity, by providing some of the same experiences, resources, activities. Doing this ensures an effective bridge between the two situations, reinforcing learning, not just repeating it.

■ Make effective use of the knowledge, strengths and opportunities offered by parents and the community, knowing that children will learn more effectively when their culture is valued.

■ Plan for and value the contribution of additional adults in their team, knowing that the work and feedback of these people is vital in effective support for children's learning.

■ Research, make and provide exciting and appropriate resources for learning, knowing the difference this quality makes to all sorts of young learners.

■ Make time to ensure their own health, well-being and professional development, because they know that CLEVER teaching is hard work!

Efficient and effective transition

In 1999, research into transfer from Y6 to Y7 found:

"The learning and development requirements are informed by the best available evidence on how children learn and reflect the broad range of skills, knowledge and attitudes children need as foundations for good future progress. Early years providers must guide the development of children's capabilities with a view to ensuring that children in their care complete the EYFS ready to benefit fully from the opportunities ahead of them."
Statutory Framework for the EYFS 2013

The same risks are now apparent at transfer between Reception and Key Stage 1.

Many of the things that happen to children as they move from stage to stage in education are linked to efficient 'removal systems', which simply transport children from one place to another, one phase to the next.

At their worst, these 'removal systems':

- Emphasise differences, not similarities

- Result in repetition, not consolidation or progress

- Make children feel de-skilled and undervalued

- Ignore vital and carefully prepared information

- Fail to involve and value parents and families

- Focus on what children can't do, rather than what they can, neglecting the skills and abilities children already have

- Emphasise dependence not independence

- Provide fracture in the curriculum, not continuity

- Result in loss of freedom and play, which are children's greatest comforts and enjoyments, and where they learn most

- Put children in larger groupings than those they have experienced, without support or explanation

- Ignore what we know about how children learn best

- Result in lowering motivation and self esteem.

Of course, we have painted the most extreme picture here, but each of these features of ineffective transition practice is well recognised!

So what do CLEVER people do to make the process more humane, useful and continuous so children do not stop learning?

Teachers already know that many children's progress slows down, often stops, and sometimes goes into reverse after a change of class, teacher, or school. It even happens within a school, as children move from teacher to teacher. This is not an effective way to proceed – time and momentum lost can seldom be regained.

The slowing down in progress and the dip in motivation are less likely to happen if transfer processes are supportive and the move is celebrated by everyone involved. Transfer should be exciting and engaging for all children, not just the most confident or the most able!

Effective transition depends on team work. The job cannot be done by one person, and it cannot be done from one side of the process. The team has to include everyone, children, parents, teachers, classroom assistants, nursery officers and managers, all working together.

Effective teams have the following characteristics:

- They are all good listeners and observers, soaking up information about children from every possible source.

- They spend time talking to each other.

- They are interested in individuals and have good memories for detail.

- They are prepared to take risks and try new things.

- They are fascinated by how children learn.

- They understand about early learning and are committed to a child-centred approach.

In fact, they are CLEVER teams!

Realistic

So far, 'Smooth Transitions' has focused on the ideal transfer process, but of course, we all live in the real world!

CLEVER people are realistic about processes, about workload, about expectations and about relationships. They realise that staff changes, new government initiatives, other pressures such as the media or parental perceptions may get in the way of a child-centred transition process.

They also realise that attitudes often have to change before practice! The people on both sides of the transition process need to accept that time and effort must be given, and that top-down pressures must be resisted. Teachers and other practitioners must be prepared to fight for a process that supports learning, rather than undermining it.

Some key factors in staying realistic are:

Build on your strengths

Before you start to change procedures, take time to recognise the things you are already doing. Monitor a year's contacts between Reception and Key Stage 1, and list all the time you spend together, the informal contacts, meetings, shared events and activities. You will be surprised how many there are.

If you are working across different organisations (different schools, pre-schools, nurseries), or with more than one setting, think of the ways you make contact, and be realistic about whether you could fit in any more.

Take your time

We all want perfect processes **now**! But the best processes develop over time. Be realistic about how much you take on, and make gradual changes towards your ideal each year.

Start early

Good transition doesn't wait till the summer term; it starts much earlier, with informal contacts and visits, events, letters, displays and information exchanges. Meetings between the adults involved should start in the autumn term, with a review of what worked well with the current Key Stage 1 intake, and a commitment to improving the process. But remember, if things are working well, don't change them!

Don't try to change things too quickly, or take on too much change in any one year. Plan a series of events over the year, perhaps one every half term. These could include activities or visits for children, meetings for adults, information sessions for parents, letter exchanges between groups of children, cultural celebrations, concerts, shows and displays, home visits and booklets.

Concentrate on things you are doing anyway, not special events. You could:

■ Invite children to a class assembly.

■ Share a walk to the park.

■ Have a spot at a staff meeting for information exchange.

■ Arrange a meeting for parents after a school event.

■ Display some photos and children's work.

■ Make a photo book to share.

■ Have a 'Fun Sports Day' or a 'Family Fun Day'.

■ Share the cost of an entertainer or another educational visitor.

Collect opinions

Ask Year 1 children and their parents which aspects of transfer worked well, and which were still problematical. Be systematic and ask enough people to get a real view, not just a random reaction.

Discuss this information and use it to help you to improve the process without losing the strengths.

Collect good ideas

Ask everyone who might have a view! Ask colleagues in other settings, on courses and at meetings to tell you about what works for them. Don't dismiss any idea, however impractical it may seem to you. Tuck it away in your memory and consider whether it has something to offer to the process you are developing.

Ask your local advisers to tell you about good practice they have seen, and consider these. If you can be released, go and have a look at the process in other schools and settings, or phone or e-mail them for more information.

Engage different learners

Children have different learning styles. Make sure you appeal to all three in your programme of visits, question and answer sessions and photos.

Remember that adults have different learning styles too. Some parents and teachers will welcome written information and photos, others will enjoy a talk about the issues. Kinaesthetic learners will get most from a visit where they can get the whole experience.

Make information manageable

Talk to your colleagues about what information they **need** and what they will **use**. We can (and often do) write at length about the children; we have known them intimately for at least a year, and we have so much information. However, the more we write, and the more we send, the less likely it is to be read. A Year 7 teacher once said of the portfolio sent with a child: "What am I supposed to learn from seeing a picture of a blue giraffe, painted when this child was four?"

In an information obsessed era, we must be prepared to make transfer information concise and accessible. Realistic information is easy to understand, easy to interpret and easy to fit with a new programme for learning. That's CLEVER teaching!

CLEVER teachers and CLEVER teams make information easy for colleagues to use – they interpret Foundation Stage language, talking through and explaining the structure and content of records and reports. They ask for guidance on how to present information in ways that are helpful to others. They combine information given to parents with that passed on to Key Stage 1 staff, ensuring that they don't write things twice, when once will do!

They reconcile 'What sending staff need to send with what receiving staff need to know', while ensuring that essential information is not lost on the way.

And finally...

This book is full of practical ideas for making the process of transition more comfortable and more effective – ideas for Reception and Nursery staff and for Key Stage 1 teachers and their assistants. We hope you find them useful and will explore the process together.

Just remember:

- Involve the children

- Talk to each other

- Involve parents

- Make change slowly

- Watch and listen

- Learn about learning

Be assertive and do what you know is right for the children in your care!

That way, transition will be smooth, children's needs will be met, and we will never again hear a child say:

"There ent no sand and the work's too 'ard."

Some CLEVER activities to support learning in Year 1

Objective for Year 1
From the National Curriculum Guidance for Year 1:

"Young readers encounter words that they have not seen before much more frequently than experienced readers do, and they may not know the meaning of some of these. Practice at reading such words by sounding and blending can provide opportunities not only for pupils to develop confidence in their decoding skills, but also for teachers to explain the meaning and thus develop pupils' vocabulary."

Word hunts

Hide a selection of 'topical vocabulary' words in the imaginative play area or outside. Give the children a list of the words they are hunting for (these could make a sentence when they have all been found).

Surprises

Place key words in a small box with a favourite character, e.g. Spot the dog, Kipper or Lola. Tell the children that Spot has got a special word for them. Do this each day and as the week progresses, see if the children can remember and read all of Spot's words.

Role play scenarios

Make labels and captions, laminate them, punch holes and thread string through the holes. Place the labels and captions in a box, along with selected props for children to use as they role play the scenario. (They really enjoy wearing the label for the part they are playing, labelling the props and using the captions as part of their role play).

Different media

Use new words as the basis for making a design. Paint them onto large pieces of paper in lots of different colours. Sometimes work big and paint words onto the reverse side of old rolls of wallpaper. Make a wall hanging of new and topical vocabulary using part of an old sheet and some fabric crayons. Mount the finished piece of work onto a garden cane and display. Make words from letters cut from newspapers and magazines. Use candle wax and thin paint to write 'magic' letters. Write in sand, shaving foam, finger paint.

Dance a word

If you can work in a large space or in a hall, write some words really large and 'dance' them. Use bodies to make words.

Small world toys

Make labels and captions for children to use in conjunction with small world toys. Once you have talked through the scenario the children can use the captions to construct a 'scene'.

Work outside

Screw blackboards to the walls outside for use when collecting new words. Use playground chalk or water and large paint brushes for writing jvand reading new words outside.

Play games

Play bingo, snakes and ladders and other games, incorporating key words that you wish the children to learn.

Objective for Year 1
Objectives for Writing in the National Curriculum for Year 1:

■ Beginning to punctuate sentences using a capital letter and a full stop, question mark or exclamation mark.

■ Using a capital letter for names of people, places, the days of the week, and the personal pronoun 'I'.

Use carrier bags, junk mail and food packaging

The children can make collections of upper case letters cut from food packaging and carrier bags and use them as the basis for a collage.

Hunt the capitals

Hide some capital letters in the classroom or outside and go on a capital letter hunt.

Use different media

Make capital letters with dough, paint them, chalk them, write them in the sand. Make biscuits in the shape of letters. Write them outside with playground chalk, water and large brushes.

Go for a walk

Take a walk around the school to see how many capital letters and full stops you can spot on the way.

Use a feely bag

Put a selection of wooden or plastic letters into a feely bag and take turns to 'feel the capitals'

Stand by a capital

If you are able to work in a large space or outside, cut a selection of letters from card (some upper case and some lower case). Get the children to move in and out amongst the letters and on a given signal they find a capital letter to stand by.

Play games with name cards

Give the children a name card. It could be their own name, or the name of an animal, bird or type of food, etc. On a given signal they group themselves according to the capital letter of their word. Re-distribute the cards and repeat.

Make capitals together

Put the children into groups, give them a capital letter and see if they can use their bodies to make the letter.

Use a puppet or a toy

Explain to the children that your puppet or toy can't identify full stops and capital letters and get them to show him where they are in a text or around the classroom.

Objective for Year 1
Guidance for English in the National Curriculum for Year 1:

By listening frequently to stories, poems and non-fiction that they cannot yet read for themselves, pupils begin to understand how written language can be structured, such as how to build surprise in narratives, and the characteristic features of non-fiction.

Work with artefacts: The magic key

This is an alternative to taking a toy home and works a little like the idea of the tooth fairy. The children take home a 'magic key' in a small box. They leave it in their bedroom and during the night the parents put a small token into the box for the child to find upon waking. The story is then written for everyone to read.

Use puppets and toys

Introduce a puppet or toy. It could arrive concealed in a bag or a box. Tell the children where you found it and begin to structure its story. Use key questions to prompt their imaginations. For example: Where has it come from? What do you think it will need? What do you think we should do with it? Here again, use a camera to record what happens, e.g. your toy playing with construction, painting, eating its lunch, having a sleep, climbing out through a window, etc. Tell the beginning of a story about your character and work with the children to structure a suitable end.

Bookmaking

Choose favourite stories and use as the basis for your own story, e.g. The Gingerbread Boy could be chased by different animals or people. Mrs Wishy-Washy could have some new animals. The Wild Things could move to the seaside. The Three Bears move to high-rise flat. Make a story plan, collect the props required and then role play the story. At key points in the story, stop to take photographs. These can be used as a basis upon which the children can formulate the text.

Use a feely bag

The abandoned suitcase; a magic carpet; a treasure chest; a bottle of potion; a magic whistle, etc. Or conceal a small number of interesting artefacts in a feely bag and use as the basis for a story.

Objective for Year 1

Objectives for English in the National Curriculum for Year 1:

■ Apply phonic knowledge and skills as the route to decode words.

■ Accurately read aloud books that are consistent with their developing phonic knowledge and that do not require them to use other strategies to work out words.

Pigeon holes or message boxes

Create a pigeon hole or message box for each child so that they can write messages to each other and you can write messages to them.

Secret messages

These can be placed in bottles, can arrive through the post or come from fictional characters. If they are shrouded in secrecy the children are so much more motivated to read them!

Today's television

Have a board which displays what is on television that day/week. This is always of great interest to the children and they work very hard at reading it.

Today's menu

Do have menus posted up in the classroom. Children are infinitely interested in food and will try really hard to read them.

Interactive message boards

Have a whiteboard, blackboard or pinboard where you can write messages for the children and they can respond to them.

Hold a treasure hunt

Bury some treasure, e.g. a small token for each child and write instructions for how to find the treasure.

Use role-play situations

Place messages in the role play area, create simulations, write job descriptions for the children to read. If the children are not behaving as you would wish write them a letter of complaint from yourself or make a request in writing. Encourage other adults to write messages especially for them.

Play phonic games

Like the ones in letters and sounds.

Useful resources for CLEVER teaching

The Power of Fantasy in Early Learning; Jenny Tyrrell
Exploring Writing and Play in the Early Years; Nigel Hall & Ann Robinson.

Available from Featherstone Education (www.bloomsbury.com)

The Little Book of Role Play; Sally Featherstone

The Little Book of Writing; Helen Campbell

The Little Book of Props for Writing; Ann Roberts

The Little Book of Phonics; Sally Featherstone

The Little Book of Listening; Clare Beswick

The Little Book of Games with Sounds; Sally Featherstone

The Little Book of Explorations; Sally Featherstone

We Can Do It!; Sally Featherstone and Ros Bayley

Child-initiated Learning; Sally Featherstone and Ros Bayley

Available from Lawrence Educational (www.lawrenceeducational.co.uk)

Storylines; Ros Bayley and Lynn Broadbent

Let's Write; Ros Bayley and Lynn Broadbent

Lines of Enquiry; Ros Bayley and Lynn Broadbent

Helping Young Children With Phonics; Ros Bayley and Lynn Broadbent

For details of prices and minimum orders please visit
www.bloomsbury.com

Carrying on in Key Stage 1

This lively and detailed series is written to help teachers continue key practical activities and child-focused learning throughout KS1. Providing topic-based work and activities that are mapped onto the National Curriculum Programmes of Study, the books will help you plan and provide an effective curriculum for children with a range of abilities and ensure that no-one misses out.

Carrying on...

Construction
ISBN 978-14081-3977-6

Water
ISBN 978-1-4081-3976-9

Sand
ISBN 978-1-4081-3973-8

Role Play
ISBN 978-1-4081-3979-0

...in Key Stage 1

Involving the child at the centre of the activities, each book follows on from and builds upon the work children have done in the Foundation Stage. The tasks are active, varied and challenging, and are guaranteed to interest both boys and girls at KS1 level.